THE BILL OF RIGHTS

BY MARCIA AMIDON LUSTED

Published by The Child's World®
1980 Lookout Drive • Mankato, MN 56003-1705
800-599-READ • www.childsworld.com

ACKNOWLEDGMENTS
The Child's World®: Mary Swensen, Publishing Director
Red Line Editorial: Editorial direction and production
The Design Lab: Design

Photographs ©: iStockphoto, cover, 2; GraphicaArtis/Corbis, 5;
Georgios Art/iStockphoto, 6; Bettmann/Corbis, 7, 21; Red Line
Editorial, 8; Al Behrman/AP Images, 10; Medford Historical
Society Collection/Corbis, 12; Jason Doiy/iStockphoto, 15; Lucy
Nicholson/Reuters/Corbis, 17; Lilli's Photography/iStockphoto, 19

ISBN 9781503809000
LCCN 2015958453

Printed in the United States of America
Mankato, MN
June, 2016
PA02309

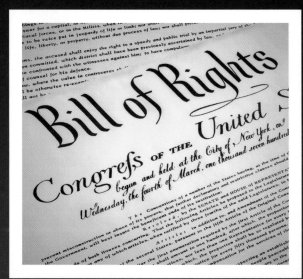

On the cover: In 1789, Congress issued a
document to introduce the Bill of Rights, the
first ten amendments to the Constitution.

TABLE OF CONTENTS

CHAPTER 1

AMENDING THE CONSTITUTION

It was the year 1787. The United States was a young nation. American colonists had fought a war to be free. They no longer lived under British rule. But they still had work to do. Americans had only a weak government. The government could not even tax people. The nation had no way of raising money. Some leaders were worried. They thought the United States could break apart.

The nation had to unite to survive. It needed a stronger government. But there were 13 states. Each had leaders and citizens with different ideas. Many disagreed about the government's role. How could the states work together?

Representatives called a **convention** to discuss the problem. By September, they had written the U.S. Constitution. This document allowed the U.S. Congress to introduce taxes. It explained how the national government would work. It established three branches of government. The Constitution could bring the nation together. But first,

**George Washington led the
Constitutional Convention in 1787.**

enough people needed to agree on it. Nine states needed to
ratify the Constitution. Then it would become the law of
the land.

Some states quickly ratified the document. But
something was missing. The Constitution described
how the government would work. It did not list people's
rights. Critics worried that the government could take
away people's freedom. Some states refused to ratify the
Constitution. They said it had to protect citizens. How could
their rights be defended?

James Madison, a member of Congress, wrote the Bill
of Rights. Madison would later become president.

The nation's founders debated the issue. They could not
rewrite the Constitution. Several states had already ratified
it. But they could write **amendments**. These would become
part of the Constitution. They would protect Americans'
freedoms.

Amendments can be proposed by Congress. People can
also propose them at a national convention. Then they have
to be ratified by the states. Today, there are 27 amendments.

States of America, propoſed by Congreſs, and ratified by the Legiſlatures of the ſeveral States, purſuant to the fifth Article of the original Conſtitution.

ARTICLE the FIRST.

After the firſt enumeration, required by the firſt article of the Conſtitution, there ſhall be one Repreſentative for every thirty thouſand, until the number ſhall amount to one hundred; to which number one Repreſentative ſhall be added for every ſubſequent increaſe of forty thouſand, until the Repreſentatives ſhall amount to two hundred, to wh'   r one Repreſentative ſhall be added f.   tv thou.
perfor

ARTICLE the SECOND.

No law, varying the compenſation for the ſervices of the Senators and Repreſentatives, ſhall take effect, until an election of Repreſentatives ſhall have intervened.

ARTICLE the THIRD.

Congreſs ſhall make no law eſtabliſhing articles of faith, or a mode of worſhip, or prohibiting the free exerciſe of religion, or abridging the freedom of ſpeech, or of the preſs, or the right of the people peaceably to aſſemble, and to petition to the government for a redreſs of grievances.

ARTICLE the FOURTH.

A well regulated militia, being neceſſary to the ſecurity of a free State, the right of the people to keep and bear arms, ſhall not be infringed.

An early draft of the Bill of Rights shows some changes that representatives made.

In 1789, James Madison wrote the first ten. They would become known as the Bill of Rights.

Madison presented his amendments to the U.S. Congress. Some representatives voted against them. They said the amendments were unnecessary. But many people disagreed. On August 24, 1789, the House of Representatives voted to accept the Bill of Rights. Weeks later, the Senate passed the amendments, too. Next, ten states had to ratify the Bill of Rights. State legislatures voted. By December 15, 1791, it was official. Ten states had ratified the Bill of Rights. It became the law. By then, all states had ratified the Constitution.

HOW AN AMENDMENT IS RATIFIED

1 TWO-THIRDS OF THE MEMBERS OF CONGRESS VOTE FOR THE AMENDMENT.

OR

TWO-THIRDS OF REPRESENTATIVES AT A NATIONAL CONVENTION VOTE FOR THE AMENDMENT.

2 THREE-FOURTHS OF STATE LEGISLATURES VOTE FOR THE AMENDMENT.

OR

THREE-FOURTHS OF STATE CONVENTIONS VOTE FOR THE AMENDMENT.

3 THE AMENDMENT IS RATIFIED. IT IS OFFICIALLY PART OF THE CONSTITUTION.

THE NUMBER OF AMENDMENTS

James Madison wrote more than ten amendments. Congress originally approved 12. However, only ten were ratified. The others were not part of the Bill of Rights. One rejected amendment was about politicians' pay. It restricted pay raises for Congress. Another was about the number of state representatives. The amendment about pay raises finally passed in 1992.

The Bill of Rights protects all Americans. Even today, it is part of people's daily lives. It describes important rights and freedoms. It makes sure these freedoms will not be taken away.

CHAPTER 2

RIGHTS AND FREEDOMS

All ten amendments protect Americans' liberty. Each one names different rights. The First Amendment may be the most important. It outlines rights known as the Five Freedoms.

One of the Five Freedoms is the freedom of religion. The government cannot establish an official religion. Americans can choose their religion. They can practice it as they like. The First Amendment also protects freedom of speech. Americans can discuss unpopular opinions. They have the right to criticize the government. Free speech helps introduce Americans to new ideas. Freedom of the press has similar effects. This right protects authors and publishers. Officials cannot tell them what to write or publish.

The First Amendment also protects freedom of **assembly**. People can gather peacefully. The government cannot break up meetings. It cannot punish people for lawful protests. The freedom to petition is the last of the Five Freedoms. It

Protesters hold up signs with words from the First Amendment.
This amendment protects people's right to free expression.

lets Americans ask the government for changes. People can
send letters to politicians. They can sign petitions to protest
a law.

The First Amendment protects many freedoms. But it
has limits. For example, there are restrictions on people's
speech. Some laws restrict making false statements. Others
outlaw making violent threats. The amendment also only
applies to government control of people's freedoms. Private

groups may have their own rules.

The Second Amendment describes a different freedom. It protects the "right to keep and bear arms." *Bear* means "carry." *Arms* means "weapons." The amendment is about the right to own and carry weapons. It also refers to the country's need for a **militia**. A militia could defend Americans. Colonists had used militias to fight British rule. Some Americans worried that their new government could become too powerful. If it did, militias could help them fight back.

Experts have debated the Second Amendment. Its meaning for people today is unclear. Some say it means all citizens can own guns. They say there should be few laws on firearms. Others say it means only people in a militia can own guns. They think there should be more rules about guns. The amendment was written long ago. Even experts are unsure how it was meant to be interpreted at the time.

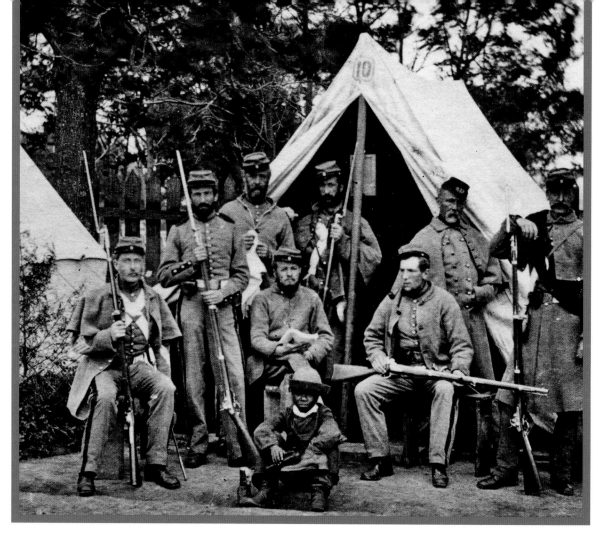

A New York militia prepared to fight
in the Civil War in 1861.

But one thing is clear. The amendment was meant to protect
Americans' liberty.

The first two amendments are important today. People
rely on their protections. Courts debate their meanings.
The Third Amendment is different. It does not often apply
to modern life. It says people cannot be forced to shelter
soldiers. The only exception is when a war takes place on

American soil. Even during wars, officials must follow the laws. Rules limit where the soldiers can go.

The Third Amendment was important in the 1700s. American colonists were often forced to house British soldiers. Colonists had to provide food for the soldiers. Soldiers could even take their property. The new government limited this practice. It gave people a right to privacy at home.

The Fourth Amendment also defends property and privacy. Sometimes, officials want to search people's homes. For example, police officers might suspect a person of a crime. They need to look for **evidence**. They may want to search bags or cars. The Fourth Amendment limits these searches. Officials cannot simply search any person's property. They need a reason for conducting their searches. Often, they are required to have **warrants**. The warrants allow them to enter people's homes or cars.

The first four amendments protect key freedoms. The other six amendments protect important rights, too. Some provide important legal rights. Others protect rights not named in the Constitution.

CHAPTER 3

PROTECTION FOR THE PEOPLE

In colonial America, many people did not receive fair trials. Some court cases were secret. People accused of crimes did not have lawyers. They could be jailed for months without a trial. They did not always know the charges against them. The founders were determined to treat citizens differently.

The Fifth Amendment lists several rights. Most relate to trials. People do not have to **testify** against themselves. They can refuse to answer questions in court. This is called "pleading the Fifth." This amendment also describes grand **juries**. These juries study evidence. They decide if there is enough evidence to try a case. People accused of serious crimes have the right to have a grand jury consider their case. The grand jury decides if charges should be made against them. The Fifth Amendment also protects people from "double jeopardy." They cannot be tried twice for the same crime.

JUSTICE DELAYED

A common legal saying is "Justice delayed is justice denied." This saying means people should not have to wait too long for a trial. Criminal charges can damage their reputations. Witnesses may start to forget what happened. For these reasons, a speedy trial is important. It helps make the legal system fair.

In a courtroom, jurors sit in a jury box to listen to the arguments and decide the case.

The Sixth Amendment promises "a speedy and public trial." People can be tried soon after they are charged with crimes. They do not have to wait in jail for years. They have the right to a lawyer, too. Lawyers know the legal system. They can interpret evidence. Lawyers help defend people accused of crimes. People also have the right to a trial by jury. The jury is made up of ordinary Americans. People's **peers** decide whether they are guilty.

The Seventh Amendment is similar to the Sixth. But it is about civil, not criminal, trials. Civil trials are between people or groups. They involve disputes rather than crimes. Americans have the right to a jury in most civil trials.

The Eighth Amendment outlaws "cruel and unusual punishments." In the colonies, people could be beaten for crimes. Some punishments were very harsh. The founders wanted to avoid certain harsh penalties. The Eighth Amendment also prevents overly high bail. Bail is money paid to release a person from jail until the trial. In most cases, after the trial, the money is returned. Bail helps make sure that people show up for their trials. There are some exceptions. In very serious cases, criminals are not released on bail. They stay in jail until the trial.

The Bill of Rights names key freedoms. But the founders could not include everything. The Ninth Amendment protects people's other rights, such as the right to privacy. These are sometimes known as unnamed rights. They are not listed in the Constitution. These rights cannot be violated just because they are not listed.

**Criminals can be punished with jail time or fines.
Their punishments cannot be cruel or unusual.**

The Tenth Amendment is about powers not named in the Constitution. It gives these powers to states or the people. This amendment protects states' role. It preserves a balance. Some Americans worried about a strong national government. The states had to give up some powers. Yet the founders wanted to keep some powers for the states.

These ten amendments are important to all Americans. Together, they protect our rights. But how do they apply to everyday life?

CHAPTER 4

THE BILL OF RIGHTS IN OUR LIVES

The Bill of Rights was written long ago. Some Americans take it for granted. But people use their rights every day.

Our nation has changed in many ways since the Bill of Rights was written. Sometimes, people disagree about how to interpret the amendments. Then it is time for the courts to step in. Courts decide how the amendments apply to today's world.

One example involves freedom of religion. People can worship as they like. However, the government cannot establish an official religion. Public schools are under government authority. They cannot make students take part in religious activities. People debate what public schools can and cannot do. What can teachers say about religious texts? Can schools celebrate religious holidays? How and when can people pray in schools? Courts consider these questions. They decide which activities are **constitutional**.

At the Supreme Court building, justices hear cases about what the amendments mean.

The Second Amendment often receives attention in the news. Some people believe in limiting gun ownership. Others disagree. They say guns can protect people. Some cities have banned certain types of guns. But courts have **overturned** strict gun bans. They say these bans violate people's rights.

People also debate the limits of the Eighth Amendment. It outlaws cruel and unusual punishment. People define "cruel" in different ways. Some think that the death penalty is too cruel. Certain states have banned this punishment. But others disagree. The death penalty remains legal in some states. However, courts have limited its use. It can be used as punishment only for the most serious crimes. Court decisions define when this penalty can be used.

How do courts decide these cases? Many disputes about amendments go to the Supreme Court. This is the highest court in the United States. Nine justices rule on Supreme Court cases. The justices examine laws or earlier court decisions. They can decide that a law or decision violates people's rights. The justices vote on a decision.

One example is a case called *Tinker v. Des Moines*, from 1968. Some students wanted to protest the Vietnam War. They wore black armbands to school. School officials told students to remove the armbands. They punished students who did not obey. Then the Supreme Court heard the case. Justices decided that the students had a right to express their views. The school had violated their rights. Students could wear the armbands. Another example is a case called *Hazelwood v. Kuhlmeier*, from 1988. A principal stopped his school's newspaper from publishing certain stories. Student reporters sued the school. They said they had a right to free

Two students from Des Moines, Iowa, showed the black armbands they wore to protest the Vietnam War.

speech. The Supreme Court voted in favor of the school. Justices wrote that a school can ban certain stories. The school can make the newspaper reflect the school's values.

These cases show the importance and limits of the First Amendment. Courts continue to hear similar cases. Judges and justices interpret the Bill of Rights. Sometimes, people disagree with the decisions. But the process helps defend our rights. The amendments have protected people's freedom for more than 200 years.

amendments (uh-MEND-ments) Amendments are additions or changes to documents. There are 27 amendments to the U.S. Constitution.

assembly (uh-SEM-blee) Assembly means gathering as a group. The First Amendment gives Americans the freedom of assembly.

constitutional (kon-sti-TOO-shun-ul) When something is constitutional, it agrees with the U.S. Constitution. The Supreme Court makes sure laws are constitutional.

convention (kun-VEN-shun) A convention is a formal meeting. Amendments to the Constitution can be proposed at a national convention.

evidence (EV-i-duns) Evidence is facts or information that are used to prove that something is true. A court must hear evidence to decide if someone is guilty of a crime.

juries (JUR-eez) Juries are groups of people who hear evidence and make decisions in a legal court. Americans have the right to be tried by juries.

militia (mil-ISH-uh) A militia is a military force made up of citizen volunteers. The Second Amendment states that a militia is important.

overturned (oh-ver-TURND) When a law or decision is overturned, it is changed. The Supreme Court has overturned laws and court decisions based on the Bill of Rights.

peers (PEERZ) Peers are people who are equals. During a trial, a person's peers decide whether the person is guilty.

ratify (RA-tif-eye) To ratify something is to sign it or give it formal approval. The states had to ratify the Constitution.

rights (RITES) Rights give people the ability to do certain things. Some rights include freedom of speech and freedom of religion.

testify (TES-tuh-feye) To testify is to give evidence. Based on the Fifth Amendment, people do not need to testify against themselves in court.

warrants (WA-rents) Warrants are documents that give officials permission to carry out certain actions. Police officers must have warrants to search private homes.

TO LEARN MORE

IN THE LIBRARY

Krull, Kathleen. *A Kids' Guide to America's Bill of Rights*. New York: HarperCollins, 2015.

Raatma, Lucia. *The Bill of Rights*. New York: Scholastic, 2011.

Sobel, Syl. *The Bill of Rights: Protecting Our Freedom Then and Now*. New York: Barron's, 2008.

ON THE WEB

Visit our Web site for links about the Bill of Rights:
childsworld.com/links

Note to Parents, Teachers, and Librarians: We routinely verify our Web links to make sure they are safe and active sites. So encourage your readers to check them out!

ABOUT THE AUTHOR

Marcia Amidon Lusted has written more than 120 books and 500 magazine articles for kids. She has also seen a copy of the Bill of Rights in Washington, DC.